EVENING IN THE PLAZA

Evening in the Plaza

Haibun & Haiku

Jeffrey Woodward

Tournesol

Detroit • 2013

Published by Tournesol Books
PO Box 441152
Detroit, MI 48244-1152

ISBN: 978-0615834757

Edited, designed and typeset by the author.
Cover image by Ray Rasmussen.

Printed in the United States of America

10 9 8 7 6 5 4 3 2 1

See pages 91-92 for an acknowledgment of the prior
publications of those haibun and haiku included in this
book.

Contents

Questions for the Flowers

Adrift   11
Time with the Heron   12
Dust Upon Dust   14
Institute of Arts   16
A Small Funeral   18
Due North   20
Questions for the Flowers   21
With a Sash Untied   24
Bright Escort—Haiku   25

Out of Season

Shorty   31
In Arcadia   34
Out of Season   36
Goat's Beard   37
The Widow's Place   40
Following the Brush   42
Evening in the Plaza   44
The Light at Savannah   45
Another Wooden Turn—Haiku   46

DEAD LETTER OFFICE

Parade 51

Family Album 52

Peace and Plenty 53

Clearly Now 54

Brittle 55

Garden Party 56

A Dry Music 57

Dead Letter Office 58

Picnic on the Grass 59

Borrowed Light—Haiku 60

LEGION

Plain Air 65

The Threshold 66

Unbridled 67

Nebraska 68

Big Sandy 69

Awake in Avalon 71

The Sweet Wild Grass 72

Legion 74

The Apple's Color—Haiku 76

Imago

California Trail	81
Sharecropper	82
The Pivot	83
Imago	84
Stone Angel	86
Abridged	87
Finis Terrae	88
Hôtel du Soleil	89

Acknowledgments   91

QUESTIONS FOR THE FLOWERS

ADRIFT

This calm? No less immediate and palpable than the unexpected storm that just passed. There's the white grain of a torn branch, pellets of hail melting at its side. Green willow leaves strewn about among magnolia and redbud petals at the river's edge. Blades of grass quivering, here and there, with the light afterthought of a May breeze. An Eastern swallowtail atop the blue flag, the shoots of reeds close by, where its wings now open a book of marvels. A current west-flowing, a sun ever brighter at the tail of the thunderheads, a former peace and order gradually restored, an arc of a rainbow inscribed and nearly perfected . . .

> a yellow skiff
> adrift from the dock
> and rocking idly

Time with the Heron

The angler will do well to set his fly-rod aside and forget for a time the alluring ritual to-and-fro rhythm of a cast, to sit on the bank beneath an inviting willow, to watch the current slur over a sandy shallow or ruffle above a rift in the rock.

Time will allow one to study the blue heron not far from the willow's shadow, to learn the skill that is his by concentrated patience and poise. The heron stalks his prey—stepping lightly upon stilts now—with a deliberation given only to one for whom time has no meaning. Even so, the heron's painstaking stealth muddies the stream. Even so, the heron pauses, stares.

Time will allow one to repeat the lyrical names of hand-tied flies—Blue Quill, Royal Coachman, Pale Evening Dun, Yellow Sally, Gray Hackle—until the syllables become a meaningless babble, having only their own inherent musical properties, like the voice of the brook before the first man came.

Time will allow the angler, also, to study that maze of light everywhere at play with the water and to gaze, without ease of penetration, at the cloudy trail a heron makes.

> when the water clears,
> the mind, also, of
> a great blue heron

Dust Upon Dust

Day beginning on a lonely byway, the two-lane county road at last dwindling to a stretch of gravel. Nothing drier after sunrise than this fine pumice-like dust with the rare car come from nowhere to toss it up, to whitewash the towering sycamore.

Day beginning on a milkweed at the shoulder of the road, a trickle of dew on a leaf now reduced to a traceable track in the dust, a tangle of crown-vetch flowering in the ditch among wild grasses already rank in the sun.

Day beginning where dust upon dust powders the sky. The horizon itself adopts the road's light complexion while the crown canopy of a sycamore pales to a white confusion with the billowing clouds. No relief in a thicket's shade from the disorientation of this withering heat. No direction but that of the buoyant orange-and-black vagrant's whose hesitation, upon the plain air, announces his leisure, his improvization, perhaps, of an advance.

the summer mansion
of a monarch—a little
farther down this road

INSTITUTE OF ARTS

Whenever I visit the Detroit Institute of Arts, when I tire of taxing my mind and my eyes with contemplation of Cézanne's portrait of his wife, Hortense, or Botticelli's *Resurrected Christ*, or even the rather grandiosely didactic but celebrated *Detroit Industry* mural by Diego Rivera, I relax by visiting those rare puppets on display from the Paul McPharlin Collection.

McPharlin, an American authority on puppetry in the first half of the 20th century, was a highly skilled puppeteer and puppet-maker himself, and founder of the Marionette Fellowship Troupe during the Great Depression in Detroit. He also authored *The Puppet Theatre in America*, still considered a standard reference in the field. McPharlin, unfortunately, died in 1948 at the age of 45.

It is no small thing to master an art, even if that art is rarely appreciated. So, again, I visit McPharlin's collection, the puppets carefully suspended under glass, looking now at an exquisite Chinese marionette, now at a rare French clown or even at one of McPharlin's own original and delicate creations.

> for the marionette
> deprived of its falsetto,
> a dream of dancing

A Small Funeral

Enough: a condolence that affords no comfort, a eulogy too feeble to enliven the perfect composure of its subject, a sermon that promises peace where peace will not serve . . .

Against fair hopes and expectations, to settle now, as one must, for the recognized rites and to commit this *being*, so precious, to a lasting rest, the homily and liturgy an obligation:

> a book of wisdom
> is set before the world
> and autumn deepens

The 23rd Psalm recited as, also, the "Our Father," the congregation files out and forms a corridor as if to wait not upon this final parting but upon the arrival of a dignitary from afar.

a tiny coffin
ventures out like a whisper
into the bright day

Not far behind, there on the steps before the great door of the church:

late autumn—
about the parish priest,
the wind is black

Due North

with the winter sun
by the hawk's overarching
eclipsed

over the barren meadow into and out of the
withered grass the ghost of my breath my
shadow

too meager
to support a wren—
December sky

QUESTIONS FOR THE FLOWERS

Siddhārtha Gautama or Shakyamuni—was it not a lotus that he held up before his disciples, smiling, in response to an inquiry concerning the nature of his awakening? So why, during the Flower Festival, is the Buddha showered with many colorful marigolds and other beauties to celebrate his birth?

Yeshu'a, during his Sermon on the Mount, alluded—not without awe—to the *lilies of the field*, to a glory and liberty therein that surpassed the wisdom and wealth of Solomon. Was it not Yeshu'a who, in one of his many peregrinations, cursed the fig out of season, his impetuous anger leading the green branch to wither?

Questions of a middle-aged man in autumn, alone at a weathered and simple writing desk, seated upon a modest, hard-backed, wooden swivel-chair, the varnish in many spots rubbed wholly away to expose the ancient grain of the oak. Impertinent questions. Naive questions.

A lotus for the Buddha's India, a lily for the Rabbi's Galilee.

The imperial crest and official seal of the world's oldest monarchy, that of Japan's emperor—the vibrant yellow or orange chrysanthemum, now bordered in red, now bordered in black—a symbol, once aligned with the Emperor's Chrysanthemum Throne, of the unity of Earth and Heaven: is there any object, beyond the Chrysanthemum Throne, that might contrast more strikingly with my unstylish chair?

The concealed Emperor on his Throne and I, exposed, at my desk—the Emperor whose family line is traced far back to a Shinto god, the Emperor yet, one imagines, counseled by that heavenly forefather—and I without a lineage to remark or an airy informant to credit.

A lotus for enlightenment, a lily for liberty, a chrysanthemum for the unity of Above and Below. Why should anyone listen to the ramblings of an aging man alone at his undistinguished desk?   Why should anyone heed the creaking of a wooden chair?

a crumpled paper
on the writing desk,
my chrysanthemum

WITH A SASH UNTIED

. . . longing without hope of satisfaction, chilly nights of fitful slumbers with an occasional dream whereafter she is drawn back abruptly to that sober, waking state and to tears, her tangled hair on an embroidered pillow, an icy silver light on her bangles, the delicate jangling of the bracelets that serves not as an alluring *come hither*, but as dissonance to accent the cold fact of another's absence.

    the slight whisper
    of sleeves of silk . . .
    a waxen moon

Bright Escort—Haiku

a raw potato
for the plain flavor of it—
the first of March

she lets the baby cry
and blankly scours a pan . . .
gathering thunderheads

junk inside,
junk outside—
spring cleaning

night
shrinks before
a spring peeper

she, too, may be proud
of her bright escort,
the summer moon

      only after my shadow
      into the deep summer
      of a grove's recess

a skeleton, too,
tugs at a tie's knot—
Día de los Muertos

      the writing
      rubbed out—
      today's moon

with every blackbird,
the sun, too, settles deeper
into the cold trees

           living in the coat
           even as it unravels—
           the depth of winter

one character
and then the whiteout
restores a blank page

           looking through
           the winter grove
           to a meadow beyond

Out of Season

SHORTY

that summer at the sawmill at the end of a
gravel county road dusty cottonwoods and
cicadas parallel rows of corn inscribing the
shortest distance between any two given
points acre upon acre so irredeemably flat as
to tempt neither carpenter's nor mason's level
the equidistant straight lines a formal study in
perspective their deep affinity drawing them
into an intimacy that gradually but definitively
invoked a proof for that ancient theorem *all is
one* out there where the hazy horizon loomed
that summer of dodging arrow-like splinters
of fresh-cut boards spit out from trim table-
saws the only nearby hamlet offering daily the
unsolicited dubiously literate admonition of
its name *Maybee* that summer of dread that a
three-foot wide circular blade the shark-like
teeth biting deep into a two-ton log not letting
go wobbling side-to-side might shatter and fly
to shear instead a man in half that summer of
a cicada before a cicada after the whining
pitch of a saw-blade adopted by the mill crew
the middle-aged sullen and balding owner

daily impatient daily worried about business
maybe his elderly and stout father in overalls
a permanently quizzical smile etched on his
pasty but red Brueghel-like countenance the
whiskey-before-work exhalation of the hi-lo
driver's explicitly bawdy tales about Mrs. So-
and-so's ever-so-easy and eager compliance
the night before the morning after whenever
he dropped by that summer when I met Shorty
in his early sixties unshaven illiterate stoop-
shouldered five foot five maybe six maybe 120
pounds in his waders his suspenders over
disheveled plaid somehow reminiscent of my
maternal grandfather his animated gestures
saying more than his barely audible his
indecipherably alien mumbling under the
mounting din of a cicada chorus that summer
Shorty for some decades resident by the
sawmill owner's leave in the property's back
10 x 12 foot cinder-block tool shed that
summer of sweat and sawdust making a hair-
shirt of one's T in the sweltering day after day
ninety-in-the-shade weather Shorty maybe
limping over a bucket of ice-water for the
crew maybe Shorty leaning somewhere along
the long shady side of the sawmill Shorty

coughing up maybe a little more of the ever present dust of the road and of the fields that summer until sundown or nearly so with overtime Shorty seated on his wooden stool before the shed maybe bent to his task of honing of honing an occasional glint from the blade's edge

    single-mindedly
    rubbing a whetstone away—
    cicadas at dusk

IN ARCADIA

I, too, would live gladly on honey and acorns, on what might be gathered freely from the groves: Hesiod, perhaps the first of many to inscribe a longing for that Golden Age, lamenting nearly three millennia ago man's fall from an earlier rustic perfection to the sophistication of a life of toil and care.

Never to know want, sickness or sorrow. Never to age but to die as if drowsily taken in sleep. To dwell in an eternal spring, to live in harmony with one's neighbor and with the land. . . .

To the Renaissance, then, and to Sir Philip Sidney's poems of frolicking shepherds and shepherdesses and to the pastoral tableau of Nicolas Poussin:

> *et in Arcadia*
> *ego* . . . with the windfall of
> acorns from the grove

Who would not dwell gladly there in that Golden Age, even though this Arcadia of the poets were no more than the stuff of dreams? A venerable reverie already in Hesiod's day? Or a lullaby for the doddering?

Outside my first marital home, there in the yard, a centuries-old and stately oak. A wife and three kids in the background, a meditation upon a looming second mortgage and mounting debts.

Listening, in the summer, to jays and squirrels bickering in the upper branches. From a neighboring house, a domestic quarrel daily renewed.

Raking the October leaves into neat piles. Watching an autumn gust scatter the leaves, again. In the early evenings, alone with a book perhaps, only the low refrain of a chilly draft through the boards of the house.

> acorns on the roof—
> in the wind, a dry echo
> of Arcadia

OUT OF SEASON

My light jacket out of season—today an abridgement of yesterday—sun ensnared by nearly naked branches, barely a glitter on the winding brook that parallels my footpath—a tuft of grass solitary, forlorn and shivering—only in the gathering dark, a lingering past, like a lengthening shadow, or a foreshortened future to reflect upon?—precious little now for water to capture and convey—kneeling, nevertheless, at a bend in the brook and cupping my hands—

coming to taste it
this late in the day
the water is clear

GOAT'S BEARD

"That's not a very pleasant name for a flower—goat's beard. Nor is *Tragopogon dubius* much better."

She knew flowers intimately—mostly the garden varieties—but she'd also studied Latin in school. Eager to affirm, if asked, that she, indeed, enjoyed Latin and held some pride in its acquisition.

Our field guide offered a four-color photograph of the plant in full flower: eight or so lance-like bracts with rays longer than the golden florets. The specimen before us, however, had flowered before our arrival and only its fruit remained: a generous crown of seeds, like a gargantuan dandelion, the feathery down and white parachute of each seed perfectly in place.

"Did you make a wish," she asked, "and blow the dandelion seed away as a child?"

I'd picked the goat's beard and gingerly held the globe up for her admiration, afraid that the least tremble of my wrist might send the seeds off upon the four winds.

"No, I don't remember doing that."

She may not have heard my reply, busy as she was with scouring the field guide.

"Noon flower," she announced, "or Jack-go-to-bed-at-noon: from the plant's behavior, closing shop, by noon, to quit the sun's rays. Now those names are more leisurely, more elegant, more suggestive."

I involuntarily stroked my grizzled beard—there, in my weedy kingdom, inviting a nymph to join me. She was younger, far younger, than I.

No trace of a breeze on that blazing morning and yet one seed and then another and yet another floated from its place in my hand.

noon flower—
the solitude of
a wish floats away

THE WIDOW'S PLACE

A widow in a plain cotton skirt, her hair whiter than the apple blossoms that she drew her hoe under every spring, there in the corner of her lot, there in her well-tilled garden. Afternoon teas with the ladies of the neighborhood—young mothers with their young children and young husbands, too, every blessèd one caressed with her "Honey," her "Darling"—and every Sunday a walk to and from the Methodist church.

Days that a shy boy brought a baked gift from his mother or a puckish daughter came to retrieve the wrinkled widow for tea. Fair weather would discover her with a spade or a basket; foul weather, on her verandah or indoors, left there to turn another brittle page of a Family Bible, peering over bifocals. Often enough, she'd recite for a child a favorite verse: "And the Lord God planted a garden eastward in Eden."

With October come and gone, with gray November settled in, one saw her less about the yard. On Sunday, however, you could count on her being there, nodding over her bifocals, in the Methodist pew, in accord with the text of the sermon: "And out of the ground made the Lord God to grow every tree that is pleasant to the sight, and good for food; the tree of life also in the midst of the garden, and the tree of knowledge of good and evil."

Passing by the widow's place on a winter's day, walking to school—passing by the leafless apple in the corner of the lot where, in fair weather, she'd kept tomato and onion and more—not uncommon on a cold morning to catch sight of her, there in her window, looking your way, looking at the needles of frost on the furrowed plot of earth . . .

> the Book of Genesis
> and, on the other hand,
> a withered garden

FOLLOWING THE BRUSH

Ink stick rubbed on the stone, the bamboo brush of wolf's or weasel's hair poised but pausing over rice paper: for Wang Xizhi, every reason to hesitate. Who, even if blessed with long life, uncommon talent and leisure to study diligently, might ever rival the free brushwork of Zhang Zhi?

Loose, sketchy, a delight to the eye as the characters flirt with legibility. "Too busy," Zhang Zhi reportedly said, "to write cursively." *Cao Shu* : the "mad grass style" of the Han master. Examples of Zhang Zhi's hand a rarity in Wang Xizhi's time, now, some 1600 years later, even the two or three masterpieces allegedly his may not be.

The wind through the grass, the brush over rice paper. Who shall read Zhang Zhi, his characters set loose to dance like the mad grass, illegible then, perished now every one?

opening the gift
of a blank book before
the sky of autumn

Notes

Wang Xizhi (or Wang Hsi-chih), 303-361 M.E., is revered as a Sage of Calligraphy and as the author of the "Preface to *Collected Poems of the Orchid Pavilion*," an essay that influenced generations of poets in China and Japan. A legend survives that he was so assiduous in his childhood devotion to writing that he blackened a pond by his house by daily washing the ink from his brushes there.

Zhang Zhi (or Chang Chih), ? -192 M.E., was a master of *cao shu* and one of Wang Xizhi's acknowledged models for his own calligraphy.

Cao Shu (literally, "grass script") is a cursive style of Chinese writing that flows freely and verges upon abstraction.

Evening in the Plaza

Cobblestone, of what former century, red again with the last rays of the sun? Elongated shadow of a sign illegible in silhouette or that of an attenuated and hushed passerby. A mind intent, in the face of *horror vacui*, upon leaving no nook unfilled here races vainly to make several discrete phenomena cohere. A tremor of baleful leaves, perhaps, or a tardy pigeon come to roost ...

> the water comes back
> to itself with a sound—
> a plaza's fountain

THE LIGHT AT SAVANNAH

stretched out lazily
on stark white linen
the length of the day

by the oriel with a Royal Delft vase and one
orchid with the lacy curtain and beveled glass
beguilingly open

paging lightly through
a summer catalogue—
the mild airs of spring

ANOTHER WOODEN TURN—HAIKU

the Garden is here
and yet I walk on—
one day in spring

        my friend only in a dream
        forgets his suicide to bring
        tidings of blossoms

on a blackboard,
the white chalk
of deep spring

        with a little rain,
        the color returns
        to a stone

the migrant has come
by a vast tomato field
to the burning sun

landfall
for a jellyfish
and lightning

clear autumn—
the name of a flower
cut into a stone

a dead tree
unabashed
stands up

an ancient waterwheel
with another wooden turn—
autumn colors

two chairs
with one table in common—
a winter evening

the walking stick
the stick of a man
walking on

thorns alone
adorn the tree—
December

DEAD LETTER OFFICE

PARADE

I am drawn along by the fat man with the stogie in his mouth, with red suspenders and pants too short for him, with his big marching drum and his close companions—the wiry guy with thick eyeglasses and brassy tuba, the little fellow with well-groomed moustache and accordion.

"Why are they marching?" I ask a bystander. He shrugs and turns away.

> a squeezebox—
> that's where it begins,
> the spring wind

Some children follow the band and two or three diminutive dogs—yapping, playful, short-haired strays. I step from the curb and join their parade.

Family Album

That's your Great Uncle with Grandpa before
the War. Which war? Why, the great one, of
course. That's Aunt Dottie and her youngest,
Ricky, with a stringer of fish from the lake. Oh,
look at this one: you! And your first
sweetheart! Didn't she have the most
beautiful blonde hair? And see! Why, your
hair is down past your shoulders, too! Just
one more, dear, I promise. Look: Dion and
Valerie, your cousins, and their border collie,
Dizzy. Everyone is so young! Oh, and there,
leaning against our Studebaker with your
father, Mrs. Flair. Our neighbor at Luna Beach,
remember?

> the clear sky
> of a snow globe
> set aside

My, my, but it's a wonder she stayed out of
jail. Heels and short-shorts! Dressing-up like
that!

PEACE AND PLENTY

> the weathered slats
> of a privacy fence,
> front and back

The old neighborhood is still what it was, more or less, when I left it: parallel rows of wooden homes, lots apportioned with a view to equality, house after house raised uniformly upon one plain but serviceable plan.

This is where, with Hitler put to rest, our boys that would be coming home were housed— they and their young families—and peace began.

Despite the cosmetic touch-up of new sod and siding or the cheery face-lift of a faux brick-front, the old neighborhood is still what it was—notwithstanding Korea or Vietnam.

CLEARLY NOW

I, too, am a master of the Way. The wind is caught up in the silk sleeves of my garment and I, too, fly to Mount Penglai. There, the Eight Immortals pour my tea.

> out of the great mill
> of a billowing cloud,
> white butterflies

I blink—a light through a crack in the curtain. The face of the bedside clock that returns my stare betrays no secret. I lie on my side like a stone, my nocturnal journey finished, my ticket to Mount Penglai cancelled because I am watchful. And I rise.

I see my closet clearly now. My blue robe, with the cloud on its sleeve, is not there.

Brittle

The grass is tinder for a fire but it does not flare. Is that the wind now or is that the grass drily murmuring? No matter. That tongue is alien and brittle nor is this Pentecost.

> why remember now
> that long ago descent
> from Mount Diablo?

The Bay Miwok escaped their Spanish captors and utterly vanished by the light of day—there in the scrub-oak and manzanita, savannah giving way to chaparral. So the *soldados* with guns and sabers christened that place *monte del diablo*—the devil's thicket.

Then the Yanquis came and then the Miwok disappeared again. By misapprehension, the Yanquis changed the name.

GARDEN PARTY

On a walk through Mrs. Dailey's garden, irises summon exclamations and tiger lilies do not lack admirers.

Mrs. Able, without equivocation, declares Miss Favor—at forty-something, the junior member of this party—*absolutely stunning* in her darling waist-cut jacket with frills. Abigail and Greta, the fifty-plus nieces of Mrs. Able, concur while Mrs. Dailey, again, inquires about Miss Favor's handsome, new neighbor.

> counterclockwise—
> the courtship of four or five
> white butterflies

The party circles back to their host's patio, dainty hors d'oeuvres, sun tea and Miss Favor's elegant evasions.

A DRY MUSIC

The rattles have quieted now. I crouch some dozen feet up the sandy path, at a safe retreat, where I may yet watch closely as the great length of that venom uncoils.

It slowly renews a task, rubbing head and neck against a nearby crag. The papery skin lisps while it peels away from the serpent's back, a row of diamonds there exposed and new, scale after scale aglitter in the late afternoon light.

> listen to a scythe
> sing to a whetstone—a dry
> song of midsummer

DEAD LETTER OFFICE

Although you may count me among that number who are inclined to say, *I would prefer not to*, midway in my journey I do not find myself disoriented in a forest but here, in the Dead Letter Office, where the Fates, busily foreshortening somebody's thread, have secured a position for me.

I often hear those white-robed and pale sisters over my shoulder, softly humming the *Te Deum* while employed at their spinning. Good Greek girls, they, too, are converted.

Meanwhile, my position is secure, for the sorting of this mail will not end. I almost said my *purgatorial business* but, in this trade, there is no cleansing. Instead, letter after letter with a bad or illegible address, with an intended recipient long departed—judgments for debts overdue, offerings of condolence, confessions of love: the destiny of every petition, no answer.

Picnic on the Grass

Toulouse-Lautrec delighted in introducing Victorine Meurent as Olympia. Something of the scandal of the Salon and of Manet's painting still hung about that démodé model like a pendant decades later—there in the red, no, the flaming coifs of hair and, even more disarmingly, in her direct, her even stare.

In 1863, barely nineteen, Victorine is where popular innuendo leads, in the Bois de Boulogne, in that urban park renowned for liaisons between proper gentlemen and prostitutes. Victorine is unabashedly nude and seated before two impeccably attired French dandies, the centerpiece of *Le déjeuner sur l'herbe*, Victorine with that perplexing smile and unflinching stare, Victorine right there for all of Paris to see.

> dipping a broad brush
> into fresh paint—
> the first day of spring

BORROWED LIGHT—HAIKU

the end of the road
but no one is home . . .
spring darkness

        a dark-eyed mother—
        thunder and today, also,
        a makeshift supper

a nest—
nothing more,
nothing less

        not a path but
        one must pass through
        the spring grass

an inch or so
of lazy water
and whirligigs

farther into
the summer grove
the sky would not follow

a shooting star . . .
then the anonymity
of a dark desire

the borrowed light
of the moon is long
upon the water

the clarity
comes to nothing . . .
a drop of dew

a mole is gray,
a mouse is brown—
fields of autumn

rekindled within
an icicle's depths—
the cold moon

the snowman
has no hat,
snow falling

LEGION

PLAIN AIR

like the shuttlecock at apogee or the
hummingbird suspended there like the granite
cliff that peaks above a cloud or the winter
fountain in perpetual fall like the Earth we
walk upon or very nearly like that

> a black swallowtail
> cannot settle upon one—
> ten thousand flowers

like the girl reclining on plain air above that
stage where the magician steps now past the
curtain now to the proscenium's edge

THE THRESHOLD

    the one small pillow
    begins to dawn upon
    their springtime faces

She smiles when she recalls him shyly plumping up the one small pillow.

It begins to dawn upon her—a frightening prospect!—that this is love.

Doves, and what of the night? There, in her vanity, their springtime faces.

UNBRIDLED

she leans on his neck
patiently, but the stallion
confesses nothing

Only, rising from his nostrils, that white
breath that mingles with hers, there before
the stable this frosty morning, when the wild,
bright eye blinks largely with a semblance of
apprehension—and she, unfastening her hand
from his mane, departs.

the thoroughbred
forgets a fence and canters
in a withered field

Nebraska

a bare tree
and then, again,
the Great Plains

opening before you as if set into place
checked and double-checked with a master
carpenter's level so nearly exact as to render
literal that old saw about mountain and
molehill frost over first light unwinding a
never-ending scroll of sky a wind to whittle
cloud after cloud away if not the stench of pig
trough pig pen another village interrupting
the prickly monotony of corn stubble another
village with a water tower's polished intro-
duction and then again corn stubble a
patchwork of brown of gray

remembering
its roots in the sky—
a bare tree

BIG SANDY

Persons are born. Persons die. Who can tell me from whence they come? Who can tell me where they go?

—Kamo no Chōmei

One room cabin—from the dirt road, two miles up a hollow by foot where a gulley washout doubles as a trail—reputedly once home or hideaway to my friend's great uncle, a Prohibition Era moonshiner or counterfeiter: the oral history varies—the county where that shack is situated dry to this day, the locals hike over the state line, the Big Sandy River, for a swill of beer, a nip of bourbon.

"Best watch your step in those hollows, son, and up those ridges"—his grandfather's admonition—"a bit of copper lining's all the white lightning boys left but their kin up there hacking, hanging grass for a cash-crop, they don't favor strangers"—then he coughed up coughed up a black lung again and he

69

finished—"and those copperheads, they're everywhere, long and thick."

One room cabin—a sag in the porch, a dusty window in the door, a wood-stove in one corner, a wooden stool opposite—little more than Kamo no Chōmei's ten-foot square hut with tarpaper tacked on, the Buddha Amida ripped away—"no one's lived up there, no one's visited that place in twenty, thirty years," the old man's catarrhal echo long after—my friend rubbing the glass with a flannel shirt sleeve for a better view into a long forsaken interior.

the old calendar
at a haphazard angle
and sun on the wall

Awake in Avalon

Fro spot my spyryt þer sprang in space . . .
I ne wyste in þis worlde quere þat hit wace . . .

—The Pearl Poet, 14th century

clouds of blossoms
dote upon the waters
and clouds of the air

In orchard or garden, by your leave, or in a
meadow but invariably on a May morning with
a chatty brook ever winding—this upon that
fabled western isle perchance but *topos* here
bows to *temenos*, where the bright air is mild
and sweet—an apple only: neither pome-
granate nor cherry will do, neither
Persephone nor Genji apply—into the water
and out of it white—

a cloudy spring
calls the ancient laundresses
to a clear stream

71

The Sweet Wild Grass

That's where we stood, that's where beforehand we knew we'd end up, a gang of boys, on a hot midsummer day, loitering about a low retainer wall that marked an entrance to a village cemetery—someone scuffing his tennis shoes in the gravel, someone chewing on a blade of sweet wild grass plucked from the broad field across the road, someone retelling an exaggerated tale that an uncle had told

Then the funeral party came, everybody in black, everybody wrinkled and dry like pale dust, everybody shuffling along in dead silence except for the muffled sobbing of somebody somewhere

      a rote recitation
      of the 23rd Psalm
      and cicadas

Then a man in black suit and tie, a lean man with a shock of white hair, approached us from that party, approached with a slow but deliberate gait, and he drew near and drew with him the hush of his black flock

But before he reached that wall, before he might come so close as to brush us with his breath or tell us whatever it was he would tell, our gang jumped up and scurried over the road, each boy then looking back over a shoulder

> going quietly
> into the deep
> grass of summer

LEGION

The landlord met me at the door to the
bungalow, and it was sticky and still, a black
cloud overhead. The landlord met me at the
door where he exchanged a key for the
agreed-upon cash. He was a fat man, a fidgety
man, and sweating profusely, he dabbed now
at his brow, now at the back of his neck with a
white handkerchief.

His property sat on an out-of-the-way and
rickety cul-de-sac. Other than the queer,
sickly, yellow wooden shingles, that tract
house could have stood-in for the white shack
next door, for the brown one beyond or for the
next white one beyond that.

> on the shady side
> of the white clapboard,
> a rest for the eyes

It's real quiet hereabouts, the landlord kept
saying, and ain't nobody asking nobody no

questions, he mumbled while chewing the stub of a big cheap cigar.

I watched him pocket the last of my cash, then closed the door behind him. I glanced about. The floors were swept clean and the place was bare. I didn't recoil from the quiet or the blank vacancy surrounding me. I hadn't come with furniture or with luggage but with a plain gunny sack and with my by-then familiar voices, the brittle voices of my dead, and they were legion.

I was only holing up for a short while anyway, holing up long enough to catch my breath, and then I would be traveling on.

> a pregnant spider
> waxing great at the threshold—
> a flash of lightning

The Apple's Color—Haiku

seated opposite
the one unoccupied chair—
an evening in spring

a headless kouros
ever lightly advancing
the left foot of stone

51 cards
in the deck
summer rain

hand-in-hand
with an amicable monster—
a child's drawing

even to the edge
of an evening cloud,
smoldering

with one hard bite
of the apple's color,
waiting for autumn

lost in the light
of a sudden clearing—
a summer grove

the voice of the reeds,
when the old man is quieted,
rattles on

unwaveringly there
with the stone she would cradle
in the clear water

      the cobblestone of
      the city's old quarter
      and red leaves

some linger,
some hurry on—
winter clouds

      the short day is mine
      by the stream that flows through it
      and coldly flows on

IMAGO

CALIFORNIA TRAIL

Often the land is level, broad and dry and one makes good time. Then there is rain or there is a trail by a thorny thicket overtaken.

A stranger, a passerby, tells of a detour to an easier route. The promised shortcut is tempting and is tried.

From a sky that yesterday was never-so-clear, what other than the shock of unseasonable snow, of those first hesitant, shivering and premature flakes?

Often there is a steep incline. Often an axle breaks.

> a late autumn wind
> over the Sierras
> to the Donner wagons

SHARECROPPER

It was my mother's great uncle on her mother's side, patiently waiting there just outside the screen door for perhaps the last time, the straw hat with the soiled band crumpled in his hand, there with the gaunt exterior of a black-and-white Walker Evans' Depression Era photograph, his skin wrinkled and parchment-thin, his voice like an echo in a dry well, his singular tale that of lean times and crop failure, of winds blowing the very land away, leaving only parched lips, only the vacant gaze.

    not a drop of rain
    since the hired hand came—
    a faraway freight

THE PIVOT

> only the wind
> in a wading pool
> and yellow leaves

Neither a whisper nor a murmur really, neither a confession nor yet a secret alluded to, but only a slightly abrasive tick or dry rubbing, an indecipherable chatter of objects within that severe discrimination of light and shadow that marks late October, of objects suddenly animated and going about their business without interest in human presence or absence, the whole of matter one vertiginous flux and one act of change where the acrid smell of wood smoke, far from every pyre or offering, lies like lead upon the air.

> the sound of a hammer
> nailing something together—
> leaves of autumn

IMAGO

even the shade
is stripped away
from a dead tree

Come, again, and visit me in the heat of the
day, that is when you always came, that is
how you always called, plainly, with your
quaint manner, a bit of stone and earth from
the garden rattling in your throat, the dust in
the air and in the sun close behind you.

the well is deep,
the well is dry . . .
cicadas

communion—
a sunflower,
a straw hat

billowing clouds
and, in the late afternoon,
a sickle's dry sound

the cicada
that does not sing
copulates

STONE ANGEL

The supplicatory pose—one knee to the earth, palm against palm with fingers pointing heavenward and head barely bowed—risks nothing but obeys convention. The figure itself is no more than a cliché, right down to the white and downy feathers that the stone-carver wished by his craft to elicit—and this from that granite wherein, on a brisk and grim and cloudy day of faint shadows, the theme of levitation is implicit.

> wings of an angel
> perpetually furled—
> the sky of autumn

ABRIDGED

This climate is too cold; this light, day after day, further abridged. The sky is everlasting, albeit flat and gray. I did not notice this on walks to school, but now—under an antique sun—I detect this constancy and nothing more.

Perhaps I should wake up in Florida, instead.

My hair is cloud-like—colorless and prey to the wind. That, at least, shall not last. Perhaps I should not make the bed.

> a green potted plant
> at the window, also—
> light from the snow

> one world within,
> one world without—
> a snowman

FINIS TERRAE

> underfoot
> each step of the way,
> flowers of the field

The florid and scholastic Latin inscription on the medieval map, with preposition added, may yet serve as my motto and destination: *to* land's end or, with true apocalyptic fervor, *to* the end of the Earth.

Oceanus, simply depicted by a repeated arabesque, encircles the known world and is broken occasionally by a naively drawn dragon or inky serpent, appropriate symbols of unfathomable depths, of what does or does not lie beyond.

> a shooting star
> before the Earth
> falls away

Hôtel du Soleil

a shining wind
throughout the day . . .
but to what end?

The stationery, with its powder-blue finish,
sits on the mahogany writing desk where the
good maid left it. And nothing is traced there,
neither sketch nor cursive, but only, if one
holds that elegant paper to the light, a
watermark that inscribes within a perfect
circle the proud name of this fashionable
hotel. It is as if a guest, by taking up one
powder-blue sheet, might fold and seal within
a matching envelope the vault of heaven.

deep spring—
lifting the veil
from the bride

Acknowledgments

The author wishes to acknowledge the following periodicals for first publishing, often in earlier versions, those haibun and haiku reprinted herein: *Ambrosia, Asahi Shimbun* (Japan), *bottle rockets, Chrysanthemum* (Austria), *Contemporary Haibun Online, Frogpond, Haibun Today, haiga online, Haiku Pix* (Taiwan), *Haiku Scotland, The Heron's Nest, a hundred gourds, Ink, Sweat & Tears* (UK), *Kokako* (New Zealand), *Lynx, Mainichi Daily News* (Japan), *Modern Haibun & Tanka Prose, Modern Haiku, moonset, Nisqually Delta Review, Noon* (Japan), *Notes from the Gean* (UK), *Paper Wasp* (Australia), *Shamrock Haiku Journal* (Ireland), *Simply Haiku,* and *tinywords*. One haiku, "the Garden is here," likewise appeared in the *Modern Haiga Anthology* (2009) while another, "some linger," was reprinted in *nothing in the window: The Red Moon Anthology of English-Language Haiku* (2012).

Nine haibun were first collected in *Quartet: a haibun string in four voices* (Teneriffe, Qld., Australia: Post Pressed, 2008), a collaboration with Jeffrey Harpeng, Patricia Prime and Diana Webb. Titles from that chapbook are "Parade,"

"Family Album," "Peace and Plenty," "Clearly Now," "Brittle," "Garden Party," "A Dry Music," "Dead Letter Office" and "Picnic on the Grass."

My thanks are due to Jim Kacian, Bruce Ross and Ken Jones, editors of *Contemporary Haibun*, for regularly selecting my work for their annual series—"Shorty," "In Arcadia" and "Goat's Beard" in *Contemporary Haibun 9* (2008); "Picnic on the Grass" in *Contemporary Haibun 10* (2009); "Imago" and "Legion" in *Contemporary Haibun 11* (2010); "Nebraska" and "Sharecropper" in *Contemporary Haibun 12* (2011); and "The Sweet Wild Grass" in *Contemporary Haibun 13* (2012). "Goat's Beard" was reprinted, again, in *dust of summers: The Red Moon Anthology of English-Language Haiku* (2008).

"Clearly Now," "Out of Season" and "Unbridled," haibun all previously published elsewhere, were kindly selected by Giselle Maya for her anthology, *Poem Tales* (Saint Martin de Castillon, France: Koyama Press, 2010).

About the Author

Jeffrey Woodward, with the exception of abbreviated stints in West Virginia, New Mexico and California, has worked and lived in the Great Lakes Region for much of his life. He graduated with honors from Eastern Michigan University with majors in language arts (linguistics) and political science. His poems and articles appear frequently in periodicals and anthologies throughout North America, Europe and Asia.

Woodward currently acts as general editor of *Haibun Today*, a journal that he founded in 2007. He formerly edited *Modern Haibun & Tanka Prose* and served, in 2010 and again in 2011, as adjudicator for the British Haiku Society's Haiku Awards. His selected poems, under the title *In Passing*, were published in 2007 and he compiled *The Tanka Prose Anthology* in 2008.

Colophon

The word *tournesol* is derived from the Italian *girasole*—meaning, "to turn with the sun"—and serves as the common French name for *Helianthus annuus*, Van Gogh's beloved sunflower. The uniform alignment of sunflowers in a field, which supports the false impression that they track the sun, results from heliotropism when the young plants are in bud. Buds maintain this heliotropic motion—a circadian rhythm that is synchronized by the sun, even when obscured on cloudy days—until, with the appearance of mature flower heads, the flowers steadfastly face East.

TOURNESOL
DETROIT • 2013

www.ingramcontent.com/pod-product-compliance
Lightning Source LLC
Chambersburg PA
CBHW032001060426
42446CB00040B/775